CW00568254

Gallery Books
Editor Peter Fallon

OEDIPUS

Derek Mahon

OEDIPUS

A version of Sophocles'
King Oedipus
and
Oedipus at Colonus

Gallery Books

Oedipus
is first published
simultaneously in paperback
and in a clothbound edition
on 27 October 2005.

The Gallery Press
Loughcrew
Oldcastle
County Meath
Ireland

© Derek Mahon 2005

ISBN 1 85235 392 9 *paperback*
    1 85235 393 7 *clothbound*

A CIP catalogue record for this book
is available from the British Library.

All rights whatsoever in this play are
strictly reserved. Requests to reproduce
the text in whole or in part, and
application for performance in any
medium, by professional or amateur
companies, or for translation into any
language should be addressed to the
publishers.

Contents

for Seamus Heaney

Introduction

The Sphinx of Greek mythology, as distinct from the Egyptian one, was a monster with the head and breasts of a woman, the body of a lion, the wings of a bird, and a human voice. 'She' sat at the edge of Thebes, posing a riddle and killing those unable to find the answer. Consulted about the problem, the Delphic Oracle replied that the Sphinx would kill herself if anyone solved the riddle, which ran: 'What goes on four legs at dawn, on two at noon, and on three at dusk?' The answer seems obvious now (the human frame); but its dramatic point lies in its intimate application to Oedipus himself as child, as vigorous man and stick-dependent sage. He's not alone in this, of course, and even his unconscious incest makes him one with mankind. 'Many a man has dreamt of similar things,' Jocasta says, anticipating Freud: 'His destiny moves us because it might have been ours; our dreams convince us that this is so.' Considerations of this kind enlarge the myth's significance and remind us that Sophocles' Theban plays aren't only about Oedipus but about Thebes, the human community. The city is stricken by an unidentified plague. Everyone suffers directly or indirectly; and Oedipus, the cause of this, will also bring redemption. Destroyer and saviour both, through his own suffering he will rescue Thebes; a new life can begin.

Sophocles' Theban plays are three in number, but *Antigone* stands apart. Though set later, it was written much earlier than *King Oedipus* and *Oedipus at Colonus*; Oedipus is dead and the focus has changed. All three have proved an inexhaustible source of inspiration, none more so than *Antigone*; Seamus Heaney's *The Burial at Thebes* is the latest in a distinguished line. The others ask to be seen as a single play united by the arc of Oedipus' fate. The story has proved amazingly tenacious and generative. There is Seneca. The famous complex shadows Hamlet and Gertrude; it is somewhere there in Webster and Racine; there are striking similarities with *King Lear*. Yeats, Stravinsky, Cocteau and Pasolini each had a go. The Yeats versions, more Yeats than Sophocles, are famously idiosyncratic, though memorable for some great lines and magnificent choral odes. The Stravinsky opera is highly regarded, and the Pasolini film is a masterpiece, one of the high points of Italian cinema. Disguised, the 'poor forked creature' appears in Beckett too.

The present version bears no comparison with any of these, but it tries out some experiments. These involve, as once with Yeats, substantial textual elisions. Things move more quickly than hitherto, particularly at Colonus, Sophocles' birthplace and site of Oedipus' death. Ismene, always a dim figure compared with her younger sister, receives more prominence and a more positive role. At the same time there is nothing here, or almost nothing, without some source in the original plays — or, since I know no Greek, in the various literal translations from which I've worked. The few exceptions are, I hope, in the right spirit.

Derek Mahon

Characters

OEDIPUS
JOCASTA
CREON
TIRESIAS
ISMENE
ANTIGONE
THESEUS
PRIESTS
GARDENER
COURIERS
SHEPHERDS
SERVANTS
SOLDIERS
CHORUSES
CITIZENS
CHILDREN

ACT ONE

King Oedipus

A spring morning before the palace at Thebes. Steps and altars. A subdued crowd of PRIESTS *and* CITIZENS *sits silently downstage. Enter* OEDIPUS *from the palace.*

OEDIPUS

Thebans, your flowers and incense, what do they mean,
your quiet demonstration and obvious pain?
I, Oedipus your king, am here to listen
in person to the cause of your agitation.
Your anxious silence buzzes in my ears.
Speak up now, tell me of your hopes and fears;
whatever I can do for you will be done.

PRIEST

Oedipus, all our citizens old and young
have come here to deliver a petition
with suppliant branches at your royal palace;
we sit on pavements and in the market-place
to ask for some initiative, some decision.
You yourself have seen our desolation,
the death-tide that engulfs us one and all:
death in the fruit, death in the fruitful soil,
death in the fields and meadows, death in the womb
and a ferocious plague blighting the home,
wasting the city to which we all belong
founded by Cadmus in his generation.
We turn to you, Oedipus, the best of men,
remembering that, a stranger to this town,
you freed us from the malevolence of the Sphinx

with your own resolution and initiative.
Act for us now again that we may live
and prosper; exorcize the curse that sinks
our health and our economy in despair.
Your ingenuity saved us once before.
Use your unique resourcefulness once more;
rule, not a desert, but the Thebes we love.

OEDIPUS

I share your grief, believe me; I'm quite aware
of your great suffering and anxiety.
All suffer, but no-one suffers more than I.
Each has his personal sorrow, his own grief,
but I suffer too for everyone gathered here,
my responsibility being the communal life.
I've wandered sleeplessly from room to room
heart-broken, baffled by the general doom;
my eyes open, all night I've lain awake
looking for answers in the lightless dark;
and there *might* be a solution. A faint spark
of hope sustains me, for my kinsman Creon
set off three days ago to ask the opinion
of the Delphic Oracle; he should be back soon.
Whatever the gods demand will be quickly done.

PRIEST

I think I see him at the Northern Gate
and waving to us as he comes into sight.

OEDIPUS

Perhaps everything is going to be all right.

Enter CREON.

. . . Brother-in-law, what word from the Oracle?

CREON

Our troubles may be over, by some miracle.

14

OEDIPUS

What did she say? What hope did she hold out?

CREON

Should I speak openly or for your ears alone?

OEDIPUS

Speak openly; the answer concerns everyone.

CREON

The Sibyl says there is some vicious thing
sprung from our Theban soil, which is destroying
the earth and must be banished from our sight.

OEDIPUS

What vicious thing? What purification rite?

CREON

The exile of a man from our sick city;
a killing is the source of our adversity.

OEDIPUS

Someone was killed? Who are we talking about?

CREON

Our previous king was obviously the victim.

OEDIPUS

King Laius? I see; I never set eyes on him.

CREON

He was murdered; and clearly the Oracle intends
we find the one who did it and make amends.

OEDIPUS

Where do we look? What on earth do we do?
The crime took place so many years ago.

CREON

Start here; the Sibyl says the fault lies here.

OEDIPUS

But he didn't die in Thebes; he died elsewhere.

CREON

He left Thebes on a pilgrimage; since when
no-one ever saw him alive again.

OEDIPUS

What, no companion, no-one to breathe a word,
to give us some report of what occurred?

CREON

They were all killed except for a single man
with the vaguest recollection of what went on.

OEDIPUS

What did he say? Did he leave us the slightest clue?

CREON

He merely reported that a bunch of thieves
ambushed the royal party and took their lives.

OEDIPUS

An outrage, and so hazardous. No mere
thieves would have tried such a risky game.
They were put up to it by somebody here.

CREON

So it was thought; but in the violent time
thereafter, the whole question was set aside.

OEDIPUS

What violence could be worse than regicide?

CREON

The murderous, riddling Sphinx consumed our days,

presenting us with more immediate difficulties.

OEDIPUS
I begin to glimpse a solution to our plight;
we'll start now and bring everything to light.
Not only have we a duty to the late king
but to ourselves. Until we expose this thing
suspicion hangs like a shadow over everyone;
besides, whoever the killer is, he might
rise up again and try to usurp the throne.
Thebans, take up your branches and disperse;
no stone will be left unturned, nothing undone
to save our city from this unnatural curse.

CHORUS
(A series of individual voices)
Thebes, the bright city, has heard
the grave voice of the Oracle
in her secret limestone cave
whirling with bat and bird.
What prophecy does she give?
We hope for a miracle
but may yet receive
some more ominous word.

Athene, daughter of Zeus,
Phoebus, lord of the sun,
visit us with your grace;
lend us your strength again
as often you did before.
Eradicate this curse;
banish the plague and pain
so we may thrive once more.

Death squats in our houses
and our infected fields;
silence of children's voices,
bird silence in the hills.
Life-loving Dionysus,

Artemis with your bow,
assist us in this crisis
as you used to long ago.

Grim scenes beyond belief,
infants dead in the womb,
the people crazed with grief,
starvation, the stricken home,
the city a living tomb:
no end to these miseries
as soul after soul flies
into night's cindery skies.

Dawn, and a toxic blight
covers the ruined earth
with a perpetual twilight;
corpses litter the street
and rats infest the hearth.
Great gods, hear our prayer:
ignite some hopeful star,
illuminate our despair.

OEDIPUS

Your prayers will be answered if we work as one
to solve this riddle baffling everyone.
A stranger to this story, as once to Thebes,
I shall need information about these thieves;
I must insist, if any of you should know
the guilty party, let him speak up now.
. . . Even the murderer, should he come forth,
will suffer only banishment, not death.
. . . Perhaps some chance foreigner was the culprit;
if so, we need to know the truth of it.
No blame: on the contrary, a timely word
will earn the general thanks and my own reward.
. . . Silence? So be it. But if someone here
is shielding himself, or anyone else, through fear,
henceforth he shall have no friend in this nation,
no roof over his head, no conversation;

and I shall insist on his excommunication
from public worship and religious rite,
banished from house and home as one unfit.
I here pronounce that the unknown murderer
or murderers, as the case may be, shall bear
universal disgrace to their dying day.
I don't exempt myself from what I say:
if I should knowingly, or even in ignorance,
receive the killer, the curse lights on me.
Your task is to ensure these things are done
out of respect for the gods, yourselves, the throne.
It astonishes me that nothing was done at once —
no purification, no investigation. Since,
however, I now hold King Laius' position
and his wife Jocasta has become my wife;
and since his children, had there been any,
I would have cherished as I do my life
and our own daughters Ismene and Antigone,
I consider myself as honour-bound to further
his cause now, as I would for my own father,
and bring the murderer to light. Damnation
to him; to the rest of us, a quick relief!

CHORUS

We are all innocent here; nor do we know
who is responsible for our present trouble.
Can we get no hint or whisper from the Sibyl?

OEDIPUS

She won't speak just because we ask her to.
Any other ideas? . . . Yes, how about you?

CHORUS

Tiresias is famous for his prophecies,
so why don't we ask Tiresias what he sees?
If anybody can help us he's the one.

OEDIPUS

Creon, my brother-in-law, had the same idea.

We've sent for Tiresias twice; is he not here?

CHORUS
There were rumours at the time but nothing more.

OEDIPUS
What rumours? Why was I not told before?

CHORUS
Some said it was bandits on the Delphi road.

OEDIPUS
Yes, so I've heard. There must be somebody
still here who was present on that fateful day.

CHORUS
Considering the sentence you've just declared
he'd be a brave man who would say a word.

OEDIPUS
He'd be a brave man who would kill a king.

CHORUS
I wonder if Tiresias knows anything:
the truth lies in his blind prophetic eyes.

Enter TIRESIAS, *led by a* BOY.

OEDIPUS
Tiresias, we know nothing escapes your prophecies.
Nothing in heaven or earth, no knowledge, lies
beyond your scope; you know though you don't see
our present discontents. We've heard the Oracle
and now we seek your guidance and advice.
It seems the only answer is to identify
and punish the murderers of the late king,
curing the city of this plague; so bring
your famous skill to bear, your magical
clairvoyant arts, dead birds and magic ring,

for the sake of these poor people here. Relieving
others is the most generous work there is.

TIRESIAS

Truly and wisely said; but to be wise
in retrospect can relieve nobody. Why
did I not remember this? I should have known
from past experience. I should not have come.

OEDIPUS

You don't speak in a very optimistic tone.

TIRESIAS

It would be much better if I went home:
you have your difficulties and I have mine.

OEDIPUS

You won't serve the city where you were born?
We need your help; so why do you decline?

TIRESIAS

Because your words can only lead to pain;
that being the case, I keep watch on my own.

OEDIPUS

What, you know something that you won't disclose?
We ask you to save Thebes and you refuse?

TIRESIAS

I've no wish to bring further grief to anyone.
Ask nothing more; I mean to keep my peace.

OEDIPUS

How dare you speak to me in that tone of voice?

TIRESIAS

I'm not to blame; attend to your own house.

OEDIPUS

What's this, you dare insult me to my face?

TIRESIAS

Whether I speak or not, the truth is known.

OEDIPUS

If so, old man, we need to know it too.

TIRESIAS

Please don't insist; and try to speak with tact.

OEDIPUS

I do insist; and now I start to suspect
that you yourself were involved in the foul act.
If you weren't blind and near the end of life
I'd say that you yourself had held the knife.

TIRESIAS

Would you indeed? So be it. The prohibition
you just pronounced applies to yourself alone:
since you yourself are the origin of this curse;
you, Oedipus, are yourself the infectious source.

OEDIPUS

How dare you? What a preposterous proposition!
Do you think I'll let you get away with that?

TIRESIAS

Do as you please; the truth is beyond dispute.

OEDIPUS

Repeat what you said so everyone can hear.

TIRESIAS

Repeat it? Did I not make my meaning clear?
You yourself are the murderer you require:
you live in ignorance and you live in sin;
your nuptial union is an unnatural one.

OEDIPUS

This is grotesque; you are a doddering idiot,
a blind and villainous old reprobate!

TIRESIAS

I'm sorry for you, mocking at me this way:
the world will say the same of you one day.

OEDIPUS

Enclosed as you are in your perpetual night,
what can you do to one who sees the light?

TIRESIAS

I take no part in public deliberation;
others will have to resolve this situation.

OEDIPUS
(aside)

. . . Others? Who? Creon perhaps . . . ? When mother-wit
and character are matched, a throne in sight,
why does envy always come into it?
Does Creon, my wife's brother, hope to replace
his best friend on a throne I never sought?
Did Creon put Tiresias up to this,
bribing the charlatan to confuse the state?
(to TIRESIAS)
What did your famous skill ever achieve?
Where were you while the Sphinx was still alive
posing a simple riddle to the city
and choking everyone for their stupidity?
A sage like you should know the right response
but all your tricks were of no consequence
till I, poor Oedipus, showed up and hit
on the right answer, thanks to my native wit.
'What goes on four legs in the morning, two
in the afternoon and three at dusk?' Would you
consider that a hard one to figure out?
Why, man himself! Good heavens, who'd have thought?
And I'm the very man you would unseat,

replacing me with Creon on the throne,
hoping to act as his chief minister.
You and your henchmen will regret this sinister
trickery; were you not an honoured sage,
you would fall victim to my personal rage.

Both of you must renounce this angry tone;
the Sibyl spoke and there are things to be done.

King though you are, you won't deny my right
to speak: I serve not you but the God of Light;
nor do I depend on Creon's patronage.
You mock me for my blindness; you have eyes
and yet you can't distinguish your own fate
or recognize those closest to your heart.
Do you know whose son you are? Without knowing it
you have committed the most grievous sin
in earth or heaven against your own kin.
Soon, exiled by a double execration,
you will be banished by your adopted nation.
Blind, then, will be your own clear-sighted eyes;
the hills will ring to your disconsolate cries
when everything is told and the truth known.
Do you even know who you are? Do you know the wife
you love so much? Your children? A harsh life
awaits you in the wandering years to come.
Invent conspiracies; bluster; shout me down;
a tragic fate is yours in the grim time
when you've been hounded out of house and home.

This is intolerable. Get out of my sight
immediately; get back where you came from.

I came at your instigation, not my own.

OEDIPUS

If I had known I'd never have sent for you:
the rubbish you've obliged me to listen to!

TIRESIAS

Your parents, though, might take a different view.

OEDIPUS

. . . Oh, yes? What do you know about my origins?

TIRESIAS

You are born today; a strange new life begins.

OEDIPUS

Why must you always speak in riddles like that?

TIRESIAS

But isn't solving riddles your special art?

OEDIPUS

You ridicule the quick wits of your saviour?

TIRESIAS

Dangerous wits, as you will soon discover.

OEDIPUS

I saved Thebes from ruin and am at peace.

TIRESIAS

Excellent; boy, take me to my own house.

OEDIPUS

Yes, take him home; he's been no help to us.

TIRESIAS

Before I go I ought to warn you, Oedipus,
that Laius' murderer is among us here —
of alien origin, so it would appear,
yet native-born, just like the rest of us.

All this will become apparent in due course.
The percipient one will be the blind man then
and the great hero an outcast among men,
condemned to wander, tapping a white cane —
father and brother, both, of his own children,
to the one woman at once spouse and son;
patricide and usurper. Think hard and long
and call me blind when you have proved me wrong.

Exit ALL *except the* CHORUS.

CHORUS
The Delphic voice announces
within her secret cave
all deaths and entrances,
the things we don't perceive;
deep in her limestone rock,
dazed by hypnotic air,
amid the swirling smoke
she knows the murderer.

Where is the wanted man,
in forest or mountain waste?
Perhaps, like a wild beast,
he roams the snow-lit dawn
hounded by unknown fears
and far from loving faces,
while in his head he hears
the murmur of angry voices.

Though none can circumvent
Tiresias' prophecies,
till proven otherwise
the king is innocent —
a hero in our eyes
who beat the predator
at her own mysteries
and saved us once before.

Enter CREON.

CREON

I'm told the king has implicated me
in some conspiracy? A stupid lie,
an intolerable slander. If the king
thinks I have done or spoken anything
against himself, he couldn't be more wrong.
Such things should not be said impetuously.

CHORUS

He spoke unthinkingly, in rage and fear.

CREON

Did he say Tiresias' story was my idea?

CHORUS

So he said, though I can't imagine why.

CREON

He claims I prompted the old man to lie?
He openly charges me with this wickedness?

CHORUS

Look, here he comes; so ask him face to face.

Enter OEDIPUS.

OEDIPUS

Well, brother-in-law, what brings you to my door?
You've got a nerve to show yourself to me,
you who've intrigued against me from the start.
What kind of idiot do you take me for?
Do you think I'm blind to your conspiracy?
Who do you think will give you their support?

CREON

This is insane; what do you charge me with?

OEDIPUS
Wasn't it you who brought Tiresias here?

CREON
Indeed I did, and brought him in good faith.

OEDIPUS
Did the old man always have such influence?

CREON
Yes, and was widely known for his sixth sense.

OEDIPUS
He was silent about the king's death at the time . . . ?
And now he charges *me* with this awful crime!

CREON
So many questions; let me ask another.
Jocasta is your wife. I, as her brother,
share palace privileges as a matter of course?

OEDIPUS
Which makes your sleazy plot so much the worse.

CREON
You charge me with conspiracy and treason —
which I deny. Oedipus, use your reason:
who would exchange a good life like my own
for the tough politics of an anxious throne?
To be a king was never my ambition.
I'm satisfied with my present situation,
an honoured one next to the seat of power:
what sensible man would wish for anything more?
The last thing I want is the responsibility
of actual government and administration,
and titles in themselves mean nothing to me.
I have no reason to fear any man;
if anyone wants a favour I'm the one
they ask, knowing I stand beside the throne.

Nobody in his right mind would prefer
a spurious kingship to a life like mine.
I tell you what, go now to the Delphic shrine
and verify my report; seek confirmation;
but don't insult me on a mere suspicion.
Disown me and you disown your truest friend:
you must be blind if you don't understand!

CHORUS

Oedipus, listen to him; he's talking sense.
Don't be deluded by your own impatience.

CREON

So, what do you think? Am I to be exiled?

OEDIPUS

Oh no, mere banishment would be far too mild;
I'm thinking more in terms of execution!

CREON

But where's the evidence for my hideous crime?

CHORUS

Enough; here comes Jocasta, and just in time.

Enter JOCASTA.

JOCASTA

What on earth are you two shouting about?
At a time like this, should you not both be out
working to cure this terrible disease
instead of bickering like two angry boys?
Shake hands and make it up, whatever it is;
the problem will look different come tonight.

CREON

Oedipus has just charged me with sedition
and now he's talking about execution.

OEDIPUS

I find he's been conspiring behind my back.

CREON

The whole thing is a ridiculous mistake.

JOCASTA

Believe him, Oedipus, for heaven's sake;
for *my* sake; for the sake of everyone.
Why would Creon conspire against his own?

CHORUS

Believe him; bring this argument to an end;
Creon was always your most faithful friend.
Don't add new bitterness to the general blight.

OEDIPUS

I think it's time the liar quit my sight.

CREON

I will, relieved and happy to be gone;
my innocence is well known to everyone.

Exit CREON.

JOCASTA

What was the reason for this childish row?

OEDIPUS

He thinks I murdered the old king; and now
he's dreaming up some means to take my place.

JOCASTA

My brother? Has he said this to your face?

OEDIPUS

They've been scheming, he and Tiresias both.
Too cunning to speak up in his own voice,
he put words into the old prophet's mouth.

JOCASTA

Oedipus, think no more of it; for, in truth,
prophecy is all tricks and speculation.
No-one has the true gift of divination,
not even Tiresias with his reputation;
so set your mind at rest. It was foretold
that Laius would be killed by his own child;
but it's well known he was cut down by thieves
at a road junction thirty miles from Thebes.
As for our only child, somebody took
and nailed his ankles to an exposed rock
so that he died there on the mountain-side;
the boy was dead when my first husband died.
So much for prophets and their great mystique:
everything will come clear when the *gods* decide.

OEDIPUS

... A junction ... thirty miles from here, you said?
Where was this? Do we know the exact place?

JOCASTA

The fork for Delphi on the main road to Thrace.
... Oedipus, dear, you've gone white in the face!

OEDIPUS

When did this happen? Tell me what you know!

JOCASTA

It was before your time — oh, years ago.

OEDIPUS

Oh, God in heaven, can the thing be true ... ?
Laius, describe him to me: old or young?

JOCASTA

Older than me; grey-haired, and his beard long.

OEDIPUS

Can the prophecy have been genuine all along?

JOCASTA

Oedipus, you're frightening me. What's wrong?

OEDIPUS

How many travelled with the king that day?

JOCASTA

Not more than six; soldiers to clear the way.

OEDIPUS

. . . A road junction . . . Who gave you this report?

JOCASTA

A servant, the one man who escaped the fight.

OEDIPUS

This servant, is he still here in the house?

JOCASTA

No, he retired right then to his own place,
and I must say I was sorry to see him go.
He's a shepherd somewhere in the hills, I hear.

OEDIPUS

Do you think we could find the man and bring him here?

JOCASTA

I expect we could; meanwhile, will you not say
what fills you with such anxiety, such fear?

OEDIPUS

Of course I will, and you should be first to know.
. . . Jocasta, let me tell you my life history;
it makes a rather fascinating story.
Polibius, King of Corinth, was my father
and Méropè, a Dorian, my mother.
I was their only son, heir to the throne;
I too, in time, would be the rightful king.
And then, one festive night, this curious thing:

an insolent man who had had too much wine
told me that I was not my father's son.
I spent a bad night, as you can imagine:
perhaps I took his words too seriously.
Disturbed, I asked my parents the next day
if there was truth in the insinuation.
Well, they were shocked and furious at the lie;
yet my disquiet would not go away.
So, on an impulse, telling nobody,
I went to the Delphic Oracle; but instead
of a straight answer to my question, heard
the ghastliest gibberish: that in the near future
I'd kill my father, marry my own mother,
incestuously co-habiting with her,
and raise children abominable to nature.
Utter rubbish, of course; but even so,
avoiding Corinth and my former home,
I took the road to Thebes and duly came
to the road junction where King Laius died.
Striding along, I met with a palanquin,
soldiers and porters; so I broke my stride
but one insulted me with an insolent sign,
gesturing rudely with an upraised thumb.
I struck him in the face; a fight broke out.
All went for me, including the old man,
but they were worn out; I was young and proud
and left them all for dead beside the road.
If that was Laius, where does it leave me now?
See what I mean? If that was Laius, you know,
your first husband, where does it leave us two?
Only the shepherd can set my mind at ease.
Laius, you said, was killed by thieves; if thieves
did it in fact, I'm not the murderer;
but if he says there was just one man there
it starts to look as if it might be me . . . !

JOCASTA
No, 'thieves' is what he said, that was his story;
everyone heard him say it, not only me.

But, either way, the Oracle got it wrong.
No child of mine ever killed anyone;
my little boy died before you were born.
Ignore this nonsense, set your mind at rest;
these famous prophets are all quacks at best.

OEDIPUS

You're right, of course; but see if we can trace
this shepherd, and hear his story, in any case.

Exit ALL *except the* CHORUS.

CHORUS

The best wisdom acknowledges
a supreme heavenly code
no mortal dare disregard,
known throughout the ages
to woman, man and god:
a code that never changes
through changing time and tide
whatever the circumstances.

A spirit of competition
inspires the generous act;
but only the despot tricked
by his own mad ambition
and drunk with lonely power
dreams of unlimited flight,
the sky if not the light,
and tumbles from his tower.

Those who ignore the laws,
who conquer by brute force
or steal their triumph, always
are punished in due course;
but the sun hides in clouds
obscuring the bright gods;
the heart no longer hears
the music of the spheres.

Real presence of the divine,
O voice of heaven hushed
in your inviolate shrine,
give back to us our faith!
Zeus, come awake and waste
our coarse materialism
with storm and lightning-spasm,
and re-enchant the earth!

Enter JOCASTA *with incense.*

JOCASTA
I have been too neglectful of religion.
My husband, taken up with fantasies,
cannot distinguish between truth and lies.
Nothing I say can put his mind at ease;
and so I turn to the gods in supplication.

She bows to the altars.

Relieve the anxieties of King Oedipus
and save us from the plague devouring Thebes!

Enter a COURIER.

COURIER
Good morning, friends; is this King Oedipus' palace?

CHORUS
It is indeed; you've come to the right place
and he's at home; this lady is his wife.

COURIER
Good morning, madam; the gods keep you safe.

JOCASTA
Thank you; what mission brings you here to us?

COURIER

News for King Oedipus and for all his house:
good news, I hope, though it is also sad.
I come from Corinth; Polibius is dead.
The people ask for Oedipus' return
to reign there in the city where he was born,
king of Corinth and Thebes; of the whole sphere.

JOCASTA

Oedipus' father dead? Quick, fetch him here!
So much for quackery and false belief:
the father he has avoided all his life
dead of a natural death . . . ? What a relief!

Enter OEDIPUS.

OEDIPUS

What's going on? Where has this man come from?

JOCASTA

He's come from Corinth; now, you listen to him.
The prophecies be damned: your father's dead!

COURIER

Dead of a natural death, as the old die.

OEDIPUS

Nothing suspicious? No sign of foul play . . . ?
What now, love, for the prophets and their tricks,
the entrails, screaming birds and whirling sticks?
The father I was to kill lies in his tomb;
my fears are nothing now but a bad dream.

JOCASTA

Didn't I tell you from the very first?

OEDIPUS

You did. I can't think why I feared the worst;
yet there remains the question of my mother.

JOCASTA

Oh, stop it; you swop one fear for another.
Why plague yourself with these imaginings?
As for incestuous marriage, mother and son,
many a man has dreamt of similar things;
besides, you're married to *me*, and life goes on.

COURIER

This other lady you mention, who do you mean?

OEDIPUS

Polibius' widow, Mérope. It was prophesied
these hands should be defiled with patricide
and I should take my mother for a bride;
so I left Corinth twenty years ago
and haven't been back since, as you must know.
Thebes is my home now, and a happy one
before our present troubles struck us down.
Nothing replaces your own home, of course;
but these are my people now, and this my house.

COURIER

And this is the reason you haven't been back since?
If so, you can be easy in your conscience
for you weren't King Polibius' natural son.
I know, since I was there when you were found.
A childless couple, they adopted you.

OEDIPUS

When was I found? Where on earth was I 'found'?

COURIER

On Mount Cithaeron, in a secret wood.
I have a farm there in that neighbourhood;
one of my shepherds brought you in to me.

OEDIPUS

Why, was I lost? I must have been very young.

COURIER

You were an infant, your two ankles bound
together, the tendons fastened with a screw.
I myself am the one who unfastened you
and kept you for a month till you were sound.
This is the source of your uneven stride.

OEDIPUS

Who left me out there on the mountain-side?

COURIER

I don't know; ask the man who found you there,
the shepherd who consigned you to my care.
He'd been a gardener at the palace here.

OEDIPUS

Does anyone know him? Can we see this man?

CHORUS

Undoubtedly you'll find he's the same one
you've sent for; surely he will be here soon.

OEDIPUS

Perhaps now we shall solve this mystery.
Jocasta, you must know about this story?

JOCASTA
(*agitated*)

To please me, Oedipus, inquire no further;
it makes no difference now about your father.
What's the point in all this ancient history?

OEDIPUS

I need to know my origin, don't you see?

JOCASTA

No; for my sake, for your own sake, you must stop!
Forget about it; let the matter drop.
It's best for everyone if you let it be.

OEDIPUS

What, are you afraid you'll be ashamed of me?
Even if we find that I was born in slavery
it doesn't affect your own proud ancestry.

JOCASTA

Oedipus, you don't know what you'll discover.

OEDIPUS

Bask in your high heredity; however
we need to know; so fetch the shepherd, somebody.

Exit a SERVANT.

JOCASTA
(*cries out in despair*)
Oh, Oedipus, we're lost and damned for ever!

Exit JOCASTA.

OEDIPUS

She is ashamed of my uncertain birth;
but I am a child of fortune, of the earth.
Nothing that we discover can trouble me
but I must know my true identity.

CHORUS

Tonight before the full moon
rises on silent Thebes
the truth of Oedipus'
origins will be known.
I sing of high Cithaeron,
its asphodel and olive,
where he was found alive
and cherished as our own.

Was he a son of Pan
delivered by some wild
daughter of wood and stream?

Was he a love-child
of Phoebus, lord of the sun,
lord of the flowery field?
Of some nymph beguiled
by Dionysus' charm?

OEDIPUS
Here they are now, look, at the Northern Gate!

Enter a SHEPHERD *with* SOLDIERS *and* CITIZENS.

This shepherd, I don't know the man by sight,
of course, not having seen him until now;
but it must be him. Do any of you know?

CHORUS
Oh yes, I remember him from years ago:
as good a man as you could hope to meet.

OEDIPUS
(*to* SHEPHERD)
Now, friend, don't be alarmed; look at my face
and tell me, did you once work in this house?

SHEPHERD
(*anxiously*)
I did, sir, as a gardener to King Laius;
I've been a shepherd now for a long time.

OEDIPUS
Whereabouts in the country do you reside?

SHEPHERD
. . . On Mount Cithaeron, sir; the eastern side.

OEDIPUS
Do you recognize this Corinthian visitor here?

SHEPHERD
This gentleman? I don't know; I can't be sure.

COURIER
But don't you remember working at my place?
I was in Corinth most of the time, of course,
but sometimes we'd be out in the fields together
watching the flocks in every kind of weather.

SHEPHERD
It was years ago; but, yes, I remember now.

COURIER
Of course you do; and don't you remember how
you found a baby boy in the secret glen,
abandoned, his feet bound, and brought him in?

SHEPHERD
What are you talking about? What do you mean?

COURIER
Old friend, there stands the baby you found then!

SHEPHERD
God, why do you bring that business up again?

OEDIPUS
If you won't answer we must make you answer.

SHEPHERD
My God, you wouldn't hurt an old man, sir?

OEDIPUS
(*indicates* COURIER)
Was it you who gave the infant to your master?

SHEPHERD
Yes, and I wish the thing were past and done.

OEDIPUS

Was he your own child? Was he the child of slaves?

SHEPHERD

He was the son of Laius and Jocasta.

OEDIPUS

She gave you her own son to be put down,
abandoned, bound, exposed to bears and wolves?

SHEPHERD

There was some prophecy they tried to stop:
the boy would kill the king when he grew up.
But I couldn't bring myself to leave him, sir;
so I handed him over to this gentleman here.
If that was you, you're an unfortunate man.

OEDIPUS

And so I am; now everything is known,
my patricide and incest equally plain.
A mother-lover, outcast among men,
I'll never look upon the sun again.

Exit OEDIPUS, COURIER, SHEPHERD *and* SOLDIERS;
CHORUS *and* CITIZENS *remain.*

CHORUS

History a show of shadows,
where is the hero whose
happiness is anything
but a complacent dream
from which he wakes in time?
Look at this wretched king,
Oedipus, for instance,
whom we called happy once.

Nobody had a surer aim,
no-one a sharper eye;
proud of his sudden fame

when the defeated Sphinx
with lion loins and wings
threw herself in the sea,
we hailed him as our own
and placed him on the throne.

Now, what a grim reversal —
Oedipus, wise and great,
shamed by a vicious fate.
Could anything be worse
than to be told, aghast,
the fertile earth you sow
received your father too?
Did the soil not protest?

Time has brought to light
as time does, of course,
the plague-making curse
of this son-and-mother
couple, once our delight.
I wish now that I'd never
seen you, son of Laius.
This is our darkest night.

Enter a SERVANT.

SERVANT

Thebans, be strong, for what I'm going to say
will grieve you in its dire extremity.
Not all the waters of the Aegean Sea
can cleanse this house of the disgrace inside.
Our beloved queen is dead, a suicide.

CHORUS

Not this on top of everything else; but how?

SERVANT

It beggars description, what I saw just now.
Running indoors distraught, as you all know,

she shut herself in her room and cried aloud
to her first husband Laius, long since dead,
rueing the son she married in his stead.
We heard her shrieking on her marriage bed;
then Oedipus rushed in, waving a sword,
kicked open the locked doors of an inner room
and found his dead wife hanging from a beam
while we looked on in shock and disbelief.
Moving as in a daze, he slashed the rope
from which she swung, and gently laid her down.
It was too late, of course; there was no hope.
So then, in a paroxysm of guilt and grief,
he plucked the golden brooches from her gown
and plunged them into his eyes time and again,
eyes which had seen too much yet not enough.
Blindly he screamed with the ferocious pain
while the hot tears flowed in a crimson rain;
and now they share disaster, man and wife:
so much for the happiness of their former life.

CHORUS
Where is he now? How can he live through this?

SERVANT
He talks of quitting Thebes, to lift the curse:
blind as he is, he sees no other course.

CHORUS
Here he is now. God, what a dreadful sight!

Enter OEDIPUS, *blind.*

OEDIPUS
I hear voices; everything else is night,
a dark night of the soul prescribed by fate.

CHORUS
The body suffers and the spirit too.

OEDIPUS

Old friends and citizens, is it really you?
Give me your hands so I can find my way.
Will you not touch me? Do you shrink away?
. . . I wish I'd never seen the light of day.
I should have been left there on the mountain-side:
much better for everyone if I had died.
Not knowing that I murdered my own father,
not knowing that I slept with my own mother,
a father of sister-daughters and brother-sons,
your Oedipus has committed the worst of sins.

CHORUS

These self-inflicted wounds trouble the mind;
it would be better to be dead than blind.

OEDIPUS

No, how could I face my parents with open eyes,
my murdered father and my mother-wife,
when they confront me in the afterlife?
The children, how could I bear their stricken gaze?
I am myself the source of the Sibyl's curse:
the people, how could I look them in the face?
I'd gladly be deaf too, to stop my ears
to the harsh echo of my sinful years,
the whisper of contempt, the moan of tears.
These things will be spoken of on every side:
in that open space where the roads divide
the very rocks remember what took place.
So great are my hot shame and my disgrace,
only black night and silence can bring me peace.
. . . Give me your hands; pity my misery . . .
Oh, kill me; fling me into the boiling sea!
Why should I care now what the future brings?

CHORUS

Creon is here, who will decide these things.

Enter CREON *with* ISMENE *and* ANTIGONE.

CREON

(*to* OEDIPUS)

I take no pleasure in your fall from grace,
nor do I charge you with your ignorant sins;
the truth was there, had we but read the signs.
Remember, though, our reverence for the light:
take him inside, out of the general sight.

OEDIPUS

Creon, old friend, I know I have no right
to make demands of you; but our Jocasta —
conduct her funeral rite as you see fit;
I know you will be kind, she was your sister.
As for myself, expel me from the city
and let me walk the roads as once before,
this time with a white stick to help me see:
having gone on two legs I shall need one more.
Ismene, are you there? And you, Antigone?
Are you both beside me in my ignominy?

CREON

Knowing how much you love them, I had them brought.

OEDIPUS

I thank you, brother, for that gentle thought.
. . . Girls, take these hands; it was their own work
that plunged your crazy father in the dark.
I can no longer rest my gaze on you;
my eyes don't see you, but they're crying too.
There are some things that can't yet be explained;
when you're both older you will understand.

Exit OEDIPUS *with* ISMENE *and* ANTIGONE.

CHORUS

Thebans, consider, this was King Oedipus once —
the greatest man alive, envied by other men
for the liberal prosperity of his reign;
who, gifted with an astonishing sixth sense,

interpreted for us the darkest mysteries.
But look what darkness, what tumultuous seas
have swamped that confident, now sunken head.
Our death awaits us at the end of the road;
only in death are we beyond catastrophes.
Think no-one fortunate while still alive;
no-one is really at peace until he dies
and takes his silence down to a tranquil grave.
Expel the vicious thing, the Sibyl said;
and Oedipus' self-exile, though we grieve
for him in his affliction, may yet restore
our health and happiness as he did before.
Our ruin, he is our saviour; no need to mourn
if the bad air lifts from our stricken town,
birds sing once more and children are born again.

ACT TWO

Oedipus at Colonus

*A summer evening before a wood at Colonus, near Athens. A road
with rocks; an equestrian bas-relief. Enter* OEDIPUS *and* ANTIGONE.

OEDIPUS

Antigone, let me sit down for a minute or two.
. . . Where are we now? Whose turn is it today
to show two hungry tramps some hospitality?
I've learnt patience, but even a famous king
exhausts himself and tires of everything.
Where are we now? See if you can find out;
speak to the locals if there are any
so we can conduct ourselves as they see fit.

ANTIGONE

Down near the water there's a great shining city
with palaces and columns, larger than Thebes.
I think it must be Athens I see down there,
its crowded squares and markets; while up here
we are on quiet, perhaps holy ground,
a sacred grove with vines and olive trees.
It's very peaceful here: no noise, no breeze
and not a soul in sight, only the sound
of a few nightingales among the leaves;
and over here there's a natural rock-seat.
You must be exhausted; here, I'll help you sit.

OEDIPUS

Daughter, your patience must be exhausted too,
guiding a doddering blind man everywhere,

watching his footsteps morning, noon and night.
It's really been quite a long time, hasn't it?

ANTIGONE

It's only natural. What else would I do?

OEDIPUS
(*sits*)
Ah, this rock-seat feels like a proper chair . . . !
Athens, you said; you can see Athens down there?

ANTIGONE

Yes, but I can't name this particular spot.
The grove has its own peculiar atmosphere
although we only happened on it by chance;
I don't quite grasp its true significance.
But I'll see if there's anyone in the vicinity:
will you be all right if I leave you here?

OEDIPUS

Oh, I'm all right; don't worry about me.

ANTIGONE

Sit still; I think there's someone in the lane.

OEDIPUS

Who is it? Somebody coming here, you mean?

Enter a GARDENER.

ANTIGONE

He's right in front of you, so speak to him.

OEDIPUS

My daughter, friend, whose bright eyes are my own,
says you can perhaps tell me where I am.

GARDENER

This is Colonus, sir, but for heaven's sake

you mustn't sit there on that holy rock;
you must come out of there before we speak.

OEDIPUS

I didn't realize . . . What god inhabits it?

GARDENER

Great goddesses, the daughters of earth and night.

OEDIPUS

What do I call them in my obsequies?

GARDENER

We say the Eumenides or the 'Kindly' Ones.

OEDIPUS

Perhaps I'll find some peace with them, for once,
since this is where I intend to end my days.
The Kindly Ones . . . A happy circumstance;
and to think we only happened on it by chance!

GARDENER

I shall have to speak to someone in authority.

OEDIPUS

Yes, but first satisfy my curiosity:
what is this place my daughter and I have found?

GARDENER

A sacred grove devoted to the Eumenides
and the sea-god Poseidon, lord of the seas;
this rough acropolis is the Athenian Rock.
               (*indicates bas-relief*)
This horseman here, for whom the town is known,
was called Colonus; the town is called Colonus.
You won't find much about it in a history book,
there aren't too many things written on us;
but those of us who live here don't complain.

OEDIPUS

Who governs here, what monarch or citizen?

GARDENER

Theseus, King of Athens; it's his domain.

OEDIPUS

Do you think I could meet King Theseus face to face?

GARDENER

My friend, you've an authoritative voice;
you're clearly serious, though in a serious state,
and an important man in your own right.
My advice to you is to sit here and wait
while I report this to the town committee.
We won't send word just yet down to the city:
it's not something to talk about to everyone
until the people here reach an opinion.

   Exit GARDENER.

OEDIPUS

Daughter, has he gone now, the man who spoke?

ANTIGONE

He's gone; there's only me; speak as you like.

OEDIPUS
   (kneels)
You Kindly Ones who frown and smile upon us,
whose grove gives me repose here in Colonus,
receive me now into your gentle grace
so I can end my days in this holy place.
Thanks for your help in my last bid for peace.
I'd die in a thunderstorm, the Sibyl swore,
and, sure enough, there's thunder in the air,
an atmosphere I've never felt before.
I expect lightning, I expect a shock
of electricity on this vibrant rock.

Dark spirits, sisters of Athene's owl,
show hospitality to my wandering soul;
have mercy on blind Oedipus' pitiful ghost
and take this broken heart to your own at last!

ANTIGONE

Some local men are coming up the hill.

OEDIPUS

Here, hide me in the grove without delay;
let's listen to what these people have to say.

Exit OEDIPUS *and* ANTIGONE; *enter* CHORUS.

CHORUS

Where is this stranger we've been told about?
He's hiding in a thicket, I've no doubt.
What sacrilege, what ignorance, to intrude
without due reverence in the sacred wood!

Enter OEDIPUS *and* ANTIGONE.

OEDIPUS

Good evening, friends; be kind to a blind man,
a wandering soul who means no harm to anyone.

CHORUS

You must come out at once, whoever you are.
. . . Your eyes, is that a recent affliction, sir?
Sit down, if you wish, here in this rocky chair.
Who are you, now, and where do you come from?

OEDIPUS

Consider me as a man without a home,
merely a man. Don't ask me who I am.

CHORUS

Who are your kin? What brings you here today?

OEDIPUS

Antigone, daughter, what am I to say?

ANTIGONE

Be open with them; it's the only way.

OEDIPUS

I come from Thebes; my name is Oedipus.

CHORUS

Not Oedipus? No! . . . You can't remain with us!

OEDIPUS

Look at the state of me; won't you show some pity?

CHORUS

Get gone before you infect us with impiety!

ANTIGONE

I'm sure you're all of a kindly disposition.
You've heard of my father's terrible mischance,
his sins performed in tragic ignorance,
and are aghast at this strange situation —
naturally so; but look at my own face.
I am his daughter; he is a man of grace,
a noble man afflicted by blind fate.
Imagine if I were a child of your community;
I am a sensitive woman and not a freak.
Speak gently to him, if only for my sake,
and offer us some measure of immunity.
At least let an old man rest; please take us in.

CHORUS

Antigone, child, of course we grieve for you,
but we must think of what the gods might do
if we should seem to condone a grievous sin.

OEDIPUS

So this is Athens' famous civilization,

the source of art and science, philosophy, literature!
Where else should we look for tolerance and reason,
the great achievements of our human nature?
Down there somewhere amid your architecture,
between this silence and the sea-horizon,
thought is cherished and good sense not unknown:
why are they available to all but me?
You shout and drive me from my sanctuary?
The gods look equally on the saint and sinner:
look into your hearts, and look to your own honour;
think hard before you decide, and bring no shame
on Athens' bright example and good name.

CHORUS

You're right, of course, and we will say no more
till the king comes, since he has been sent for.

OEDIPUS

Do you think he'll come in person to see me here?

CHORUS

I'm sure he will when he hears who you are.

OEDIPUS

And how will he know that if we haven't met?

CHORUS

News travels fast; the word is already out.

OEDIPUS

May he come soon; we've much to talk about.

ANTIGONE

Good heavens, can my eyes be playing tricks?
Back down the road, riding between the rocks,
our own Ismene, under a straw hat,
smiling and waving at us; it's her, all right!

OEDIPUS
Ismene, here? I can't believe my ears!

Enter ISMENE.

ISMENE
So here you are; I've found you at last, my dears,
and now I can scarcely make you out for tears!

OEDIPUS
It's good to hear your voice, Ismene, love:
how clever of you to find us in this grove!

ISMENE
I was heartbroken, thinking you both were lost;
besides, I have some complicated news.
I came with the one servant I can trust.

OEDIPUS
One servant? Your brothers let you travel without . . . ?

ISMENE
My brothers, yes, that's what I've come to talk about.

OEDIPUS
They've grown degenerate in my absence, then,
preoccupied with interior decoration
while women do the work once done by men?
Instead of striving for my restoration
they lie around the house and let their sisters
take on the job of handling these disasters?
Antigone here, devoted and clear-eyed,
has been my indispensable nurse and guide;
constant companion in a hostile world,
she too has walked the roads, hungry and cold,
heroic in rain and dust, without complaint,
giving me consolation and encouragement;
and you, Ismene, slipping out in disguise,
have kept us up to date with the latest news,

knowing how much your banished father grieves.
So what's the story? Any word from Thebes?

ISMENE

It took me ages to find you this time round —
and what a frightful trip! But never mind;
I'm here at last, as you see, with my loved ones.
I came post-haste so you should hear the truth
not indirectly but from my own mouth.
My darling brothers, your 'devoted' sons,
hot-heads the pair of them, have had a row
with Creon, who has banished them from the state
so that they live, like you, in exile now.
They're hiding separately on the Argive plain,
both hostile and suspicious of each other,
each with an army of a thousand men
and hoping to re-invade when the time is right.
I wish I'd happier news to give you, father.

OEDIPUS

And how is Creon handling this bit of bother?

ISMENE

He wants you back, to bring all sides together.

OEDIPUS

He wants me back to keep an eye on me.
Do the boys know about this curious plan?

ISMENE

Oh yes, but they would rather prepare for war.
There's talk of some conspiracy, some intrigue;
it's said they're forming an Achaean league
with five more sportsmen, the aim being to march
on the Seven Gates and put Thebes to the torch.

OEDIPUS

What, seven against Thebes? So they would rather
reign in a ruin than reclaim their father?

If so, let their rivalry be long and vile.
What have they done to help me in my exile?
Has either of them lifted a finger? No,
nor tried to renew contact. Only you two,
my daughters, have shown proper filial love
and what great heroism you are capable of.
My own sons making mischief behind my back?
No good will come of that, we can be sure.
I want nothing to do with this wicked war:
fight as they will, I wish them both bad luck.
Though Thebes come after me, this sacred grove
remains my refuge and my sanctuary
if heaven permits, and if it will receive me.
Hardship has given me supernatural power;
I exercise a new mystical authority.
Athens will benefit from my presence here.

CHORUS

We want to help you, Oedipus, in Colonus;
so rest assured you can rely upon us.
Will you please now listen to what we advise?

OEDIPUS

Of course I will; I'm sure it's for the best.

CHORUS

We need to set the Kindly Ones at rest;
you must at once appease the deities
whose rules you broke on your first coming here.

OEDIPUS

You'd better show me how to put this right.
What must I do? Is there some special rite?

CHORUS

Ismene, can you show him? He has to bring
a bowl of water from this holy spring
and pour it out, his face to the evening light.
Pour once, twice; and a third time, that's right;

empty the pitcher into the thirsty soil,
imploring the Kindly Ones to save your soul.
. . . Now, harsh though it be to open an old wound,
we want to ask you how you came to be blind.
We've heard wild rumours about Oedipus:
will you not set the record straight for us?
I see this is hard for you, so take your time.

OEDIPUS

Don't think me guilty of a deliberate crime.
Blindly, unknowingly, I slew my father
by purest chance, and married my own mother,
his wife, who took her life when the truth was known.
I couldn't bear to look upon what I'd done
so I tore out my eyes in grief and shame.

CHORUS

Each child is your own sister, your own brother?

OEDIPUS

Yes, I'm afraid we're all in this together.

CHORUS

Of all the dire things this is the direst thing.
But someone's in the lane; here comes the king.

Enter THESEUS *and* SOLDIERS.

THESEUS

. . . Oedipus, yes, your story is one I know.
Who doesn't? It must be several years ago
we heard you were cast out from your own hearth
and self-condemned to live on the open heath.
Your blind eyes, your demeanour, your ragged cloth
convince me you really are that ruined king.
Unfortunate Oedipus, is there anything
you wish to ask of Athens or of me?
I consider myself unshockable; speak openly.
I too know about exile and adversity

and won't refuse you refuge in our city.
You will receive here nothing but respect.
I'm only a man myself. Who knows what act
of fate may strip *me* of my throne and power?
None of us knows what fortune holds in store.
So tell me now, what brings you here to me?
Thebes seems the obvious place for you to be.

OEDIPUS

Oh no, I shall never set foot in Thebes again.
Banished by my own family, my own men,
the past rules out all thought of restoration;
I see no hope of reconciliation.
But they will come to use me in their games;
they want my sanction for their warlike aims.
Even here we're not safe from their stratagems.

THESEUS

What friction could ever arise between our cities?

OEDIPUS

Who knows what unpredictable animosities,
what changing times or personal ambitions
may threaten our traditional good relations?
The sun shines here on this Athenian Rock;
but much can happen in a year, a week.
Somewhere along the road a hair-line crack,
opening up and growing, could mean a break
and put an end to our best resolutions;
then fire and sword, the lunacy of war.
As for myself, I know my place is here.

THESEUS

Oedipus, I agree to your frank demand.
Welcome to Athens; here, give me your hand
and make yourself at home as you think best.
Come down to the city as my special guest
or stay here in Colonus where you can rest.
You will be safe here, and your daughters too;

these fine people will take good care of you.

OEDIPUS

Theseus, thank you for your generosity.

THESEUS

So come and stay with us in our great city;
you'll find a new enlightenment down there
with drama and philosophy in the air.

OEDIPUS

Thanks, but I'm my own best philosopher;
for me, amusements are a thing of the past.
This is the place for me; I must stay here.

THESEUS

As you prefer; you know what you have to do.
Trust me; I don't renegue on solemn promises.
Get strong here in these sacred premises.
You've been a long time among dust and stones
but here you're in the hands of the Kindly Ones
who will protect you with their magic powers
and watch you, owl-like, during the long night hours.
You need have no fear of your Theban friends,
whose strength bears no comparison with ours.
I'll leave you now, but leave you in good hands.

Exit THESEUS *and* SOLDIERS.

CHORUS

This here is Colonus' glittering town
known everywhere for horses, known
for its fine ships, where nightingales
sing in our quiet glades and hills,
the warm peace of our ivy glens,
in arbours hung with fruit and vines
out of the burning sun, and glimpse
the goat-god with his naked nymphs.

Washed in the dew of morning skies,
grave asphodels with shining eyes
sprinkle the forest floor and bright
crocuses blink in shafts of light.
Sparkling springs bubble and boil
down to the fields and drinking soil,
nourishing with their ample flow
the rich loins of the earth below.

With song and dance the Muses thrive
and teach the people how to live;
the dark-eyed olive flourishes here
in greater abundance than elsewhere,
its shade the school each student knows,
its woods a shield against our foes,
self-sown, self-grown and self-reliant,
watched by Athene day and night.

The horse, though, is our chief resource,
Poseidon's gift to us, the horse
and the white horses of the sea
we tamed here in our infancy
with bit and bridle, sail and oar,
on the high-road and foaming shore;
and still we ride the salt sea-wind
as in the first days of mankind.

Enter CREON *and* SOLDIERS.

CREON

A fortunate spot indeed . . . I come in peace —
there's no need for resistance or abuse,
no reason for alarm, no cause to hide.
I know we're in King Theseus' countryside;
and very nice it is, with its woods and glebes.
No doubt you wonder what I'm doing here?
I need our ex-king to return to Thebes.
Oedipus, time to come home; we need you there,
we need you as we needed you once before.

We ask you to forgive, to rest and thrive,
not walk the roads like a tramp or fugitive.
At least think of your daughters; think of young
Antigone, self-condemned to be your guide.
She was always vulnerable, she is not strong:
when will we see her as a blushing bride?
Brother, come home with me; Thebes wants you back.
Thank these good people, who have shown such tact,
and come: your exile has gone on too long.

OEDIPUS

You've changed . . . Where is the sensible Creon now?
You snap like somebody I hardly know.
I may be blind, though not to your obvious tricks.
This isn't family feeling; this is politics.
You track me down so you can use my name
and influence in some new strategic game;
you're not here, are you, out of consideration
but from some diplomatic calculation;
you're not here out of the kindness of your heart
but because you want me as a pawn, some sort
of token, talisman, am I not right?
Oh, I see through your schemes. Out of my sight!
Go back the way you came; leave me in peace.

CREON

You might have answered with a better grace;
you're cutting off your nose to spite your face.
But there's a trump card I have yet to play.
Men, seize the daughters; take them both away!

CHORUS

You daren't; these visitors have immunity
within the confines of King Theseus' city.

CREON'S SOLDIERS *seize* ISMENE *and* ANTIGONE.

ISMENE

Take your hands off me, you sadistic scum!

CREON

You keep the father; I have the daughters. Come!

CHORUS

This is outrageous; this is an act of war!
Release them or, armed only as we are,
we shall resist with all means in our power.

CREON

Oh yes? Bravely said, but I don't think so.
. . . I want these women bound from top to toe.
There's no more to be said; it's time to go.

Exit CREON'S SOLDIERS *with* ISMENE *and* ANTIGONE;
enter THESEUS *and* SOLDIERS.

THESEUS

What's going on? I'm making sacrifices
to the sea-god when I hear the sound of voices
raised in anger. Was that a fight I heard?

OEDIPUS

Theseus, listen, this is a border raid —
a bunch of Theban soldiers have just made
off with my daughters down to the main road.
Creon here is responsible for all this.

THESEUS

I want a whole division on their track.
Beat off the Thebans; bring the women back!

Exit SOLDIERS; *to* CREON

. . . How dare you come here and impose on us?
Don't you know where you are? This is Colonus,
sacred to both Poseidon and Athene.
This grove houses our tutelary deities,
the Eumenides you've heard of, and if any
stranger like you bursts in with impudent eyes,

hoping to take our people by surprise,
you'll find more trouble than you realize.
You can't march in and bear off any prize
that takes your fancy. What of the decencies?
Your people would be ashamed of you. I know
Thebes, a fine place; but you're in Athens now.
A man of your age and experience
should know how to behave; have you no sense?
I want the girls back here immediately
or you remain a hostage here with me.
Take notice, now; I mean this seriously.

CREON

Theseus, I've no quarrel with you, although
I'm rather taken aback by your insistence
on giving refuge to an incestuous patricide.
Athenian practice, and you have your reasons,
grants no asylum to such dangerous persons,
so I felt within my rights to trace him here,
even at the risk of breaching your frontier.
I come to offer him a safe return;
he greets me with suspicion, pride and scorn.

OEDIPUS

Theseus puts you on your best behaviour.
You come here looking for his grace and favour
and praising his wise government to the skies;
here you are, pretending to be my saviour,
and trampling stupidly upon holy ground
like some barbarian ignorant of the niceties.
Athens owes her distinction on this earth
to a true love of the gods who brought her forth;
but you come blundering into their sacred space
to abduct my daughters and destroy my peace.
I ask the Kind Ones, in whose grove you are,
to back the Athenians if it comes to war!

THESEUS

While we stand talking the raiders are half-way home.

Creon and I will ride out, intercept them
and bring your daughters safely back to you.
Athens won't stand for this sort of invasion
and, when we choose, we are a fighting nation.
We'll negotiate an exchange of prisoners
and if that doesn't work, so much the worse!

Exit THESEUS, CREON *and* SOLDIERS.

CHORUS
The perverse thrill of war —
glitter of lance and shield,
concert of sword and spear
as the mild buzzard gazes
on a hot, furious field
or a sun-dazzled shore
where upon summer days
the bright weapons glare.

Theseus will be found where
the fighting is most intense
and the death-wind whirls
with greatest violence;
out there he will recover
the two frightened girls,
proxies for their father,
and bring them safely here.

Jingling with bit and bridle,
taking the coastal road,
Colonus' young men ride
with Theseus' soldiery
watched over by grey-eyed
Athene and old Poseidon,
trident and dripping beard,
earth-shaker, lord of the sea.

O for the wings of a dove
to flutter and fly above

the clouds and the dust-clouds
with wide panoptic eye!
We shall prevail, the gods
are with us; we shall see
Ismene and Antigone
restored to their father's love.

. . . All quiet; the king is coming up the road
with your two daughters safely at his side.

Enter THESEUS, ISMENE *and* ANTIGONE.

OEDIPUS

Where are you? Are you there? Are you all right?

ISMENE

We're fine now, after our initial fright.

Distant thunder.

OEDIPUS

Now listen, there's the sign, the time has come;
the gods are calling me to my final home.
I can almost feel my way; come on, Antigone,
let's go; this is as good a time as any.
The lightning . . . It's a long time now since I
looked up in wonder at the changing sky;
so many years with no light in my head.
What more I have to say, I'll share it with the dead.

Exit upstage OEDIPUS, THESEUS, ISMENE, ANTIGONE
and GARDENER.

CHORUS

While a white sea rinses
the coast and the coast road,
like one come to his senses
he goes to the dark wood;
with bird-song in his ears

and the leaves listening,
perhaps he even hears
the blue water glistening.

No sane person resents
the natural life sentence,
for where lies the advantage
in a prolonged old age,
decrepitude and pain?
Death comes to everyone;
no music, no song and dance
can check our last decline.

Best not to have been born;
next best, a brisk return
to the pre-natal night.
When once our youth is past
griefs come thick and fast:
rancour, reproach and spite,
not many we can trust
and the mind gone at last.

This is the general fate;
Oedipus' too, of course —
who morning, noon and night,
like a storm-beaten cliff
in distant northern seas,
weathered the bitter blows
that broke over his life;
and are they finished yet?

Thunder and lightning. Re-enter GARDENER, THESEUS,
ISMENE *and* ANTIGONE.

ISMENE
He's gone; between the chasm and the rock stairs
he paused a bit between the wooden banisters,
such thunder in the sky we were scared stiff
as if the whole earth might implode; as if

the gods themselves had made some fateful vow.
We screamed aloud and, really frightened now,
clung childishly to our old father's knees
while he, clutching us as we clung there,
said, 'This is the last of your responsibilities;
it was hard, I know,' said he, 'but the end is here.
One thing consoles us this side of the grave
and even beyond it, and that thing is love.
But now I'm called for; the immortal gods
wait patiently beyond the thunder-clouds.
Your love sustained me while I was alive;
now you must find some other way to live.'
Suddenly, to our amazement, we heard a voice,
a god-voice speaking from above the storm:
'Oedipus,' it announced, 'the time has come.'
He vanished as if drawn into a cloud
or the earth opened and closed above his head.

ANTIGONE

While he was alive we helped him bear the pain
of his own fate and our strange origin.

ISMENE

Now we are left to face these things alone —
as much in the dark, it seems, as he was then.

CHORUS

You girls are innocent of any crime.

ANTIGONE

I never thought that there would come a time
when I would weep for a lost martyrdom.
There was defiance, there was perverse pride,
even in misery, at our father's side.

ISMENE

What will become of us with our father dead?

68

THESEUS

Now, no more tears; he died a gentle death
and lies in his own chosen piece of earth.

ANTIGONE

So be it, Theseus; but from this grove
now send us home to the Thebes we fear and love.
Enough of sacrifice, enough of grief;
it's time now to get on with a new life.
While we stand amiably conversing here
our stupid brothers have prepared for war;
perhaps we can put an end to their pointless strife.

CHORUS

Oedipus lies at peace in his dark tomb
and so remains now and in time to come.
This was a chronicle of despair and grace;
whatever the future, nothing can now replace
the fierce integrity of its taking place.
Be it disastrous, tragic or sublime,
what happens once has happened for all time.

It grows dark; a nightingale sings; cry of a new-born child.